A SIMPLE CUP OF -TY

BY ELDA ROBINSON
Photographs by Andy Robinson

A SIMPLE CUP OF -TY

Sea Mist Imaginations

ISBN 978-1-7375752-1-4 (paperback)
ISBN 978-1-7375752-0-7 (hardcover)

Printed in the United States of America.

WHAT PEOPLE ARE SAYING

"You'll want to read its interactive pages again and again..."
—Shelby Kottemann, author of *Evolution of a Soul*

"You will be enriched and inspired!"
—Donny Ingram, author of *Real Freedom*

"Like a perfect cup of tea..."
—Maureen Ryan Blake, founder of the Power of the Tribe Network

"A *Simple Cup of -Ty* is the perfect volume of whimsical musings and daily inspirations..."
—Aeriol Ascher, author/coach

"A delightful way to start or end your day..."
—Wendy K. Benson and Elizabeth A. Myers, co-Authors of *The Confident Patient*

CONTENTS

DEDICATION AND ACKNOWLEDGEMENTS

THIS BOOK IS DEDICATED to my cousin/sister, Tricia Emory. My family all agree that Tricia was our sister by love. She attended a lot of our family reunions, helped close out the family farm, counseled us, encouraged us, and loved us without restraint.

She loved tea and I am sure would love the play on words for this book. It is my prayer that her family understands the honor and love we still have for her.

I want to acknowledge my family and friends who encouraged me to go beyond just doing something for the family to see. It has taken quite a few years to finally be able to do this! Thanks also to those friends who read the drafts.

Special love and acknowledgement goes to my husband, Andy. He did the photography for this as well as read numerous drafts. He is an awesome man and I love him. We make a great team and have for 50 years. Some of the photographs are from my personal collection, but I want to say a special thanks to my neighbor, Eva. Her beautiful collection of teacups and teapots from around the world were a great help.

The cover shot is a cup my Dad used when I was growing up. It is made by Corning. Dad surprised guests by throwing the empty cup across the kitchen floor because it was advertised not to break. It never did!

ANIMOSITY

"Life appears to me too short to be spent in nursing animosity, or registering wrongs."
—Charlotte Brontë

WHAT DOES ANIMOSITY MEAN? According to the dictionary, it means "a strong feeling of dislike or hatred: ill will or resentment tending toward active hostility." Can't you just feel that animosity in the words? What a way to live your life.

I decided to do a little research about animosity. Interestingly, the first two pages of articles that came up from my Google search were about consumer animosity—not buying a product because of its origin. That was a different way of thinking about it! We won't buy products from a specific country because it is THAT country. We won't buy _____ because my family never buys that.

But I was thinking more about the personal effects. Eventually I found an article from the University of Minnesota that was contributed by Karen Lawson MD. It's a short, easy read essay that outlines the negative effects of animosity. The list isn't even that long: chronic stress; hormone imbalance; damage to immune system; decrease of lifespan; hypertension; cardiovascular disease; infection and digestive disorders. That's quite a list! Imagine the effect on your body, your lifestyle, and your relationships. It seems like nothing good comes from animosity.

But it must, then, be replaced by something else. So I looked up the antonym, and there is a whole list! Two of them seemed most applicable: goodwill and kindness. Both of these involve going beyond whatever prejudices we may have and looking for a way to help another person. In essence, that would be thinking outside YOUR box!

So, I challenge you to lay down those long held animosities, clear your mind of paralyzing thoughts of revenge, and look at how you could be kind and good. It doesn't have to be anything big. Smile at the check-out lady or thank the mail carrier. Maybe you will become just like the Grinch, and your heart will begin to grow.

REFLECTION QUESTIONS

Do you have animosity toward another? What are some first steps you need to take?

CERTAINTY

"Listen to Mustn'ts, child, listen to the Don'ts. Listen to the Shouldn'ts, the Impossibles, the Won'ts. Listen to the Never Haves, then listen close to me. Anything can happen, child, Anything can be."
—*Shel Silverstein*

THE CERTAINTY OF YOUTH can become the uncertainty of the mature. Young people are so sure they know, that they can do and accomplish without doubt.

Maturity can bring the ability to see all sides of an issue before a decision is made. That perspective can help in making wise choices. However, it can also bring the fear of making any choice and remaining stuck or stagnant. And everyone knows a stagnant pond smells!

It doesn't have to be a big thing. How about trying a new food you aren't sure of? My husband wasn't sure about eating tacos when he first came to the West coast. Now he is a true believer!

Maturity can also bring sadness when faced with the realization that one may never be able to accomplish all their dreams and goals. But it is a certainty that they never will be reached unless tried. We should be individuals who refuse to listen to what Shel Silverstein calls "the mustn'ts." Marvelous things can be accomplished no matter what age with a little certainty.

REFLECTION QUESTIONS

What is something you aren't certain of but will try anyway?
What happened when you tried it?

CHOCOLATEY

IRST, THERE IS THE RICH, intense dark chocolate. The hint of bitterness enhances the deep flavor that evokes memories of dark forests and hidden ponds. This chocolate is made to be savored. Sometimes life is like dark chocolate. It is intense, and often accompanied with bitterness. Take time to savor these experiences. Use them to learn more about yourself. Evaluate your direction and see if you need to make changes. Realize you are strong enough to deal with whatever you are currently going through.

Second is the smooth, softer essence that milk chocolate gives. It melts in your mouth and reminds one of Mom's Christmas fudge. There is no bitterness in this type of chocolate. Sometimes life is like the sweetness of milk chocolate. Things are going well and there are no issues. Don't rush through these times. Enjoy them to the fullest, and remember them when life gets more complicated.

Many chocolate purists insist that white chocolate isn't really chocolate. It doesn't have the full bodied flavor of dark chocolate or the sweet, gentle taste of milk chocolate. It has a unique, unexpected flavor all its own. White chocolate reminds us of the totally unexpected things in life. These moments that take our breath away, leave us in awe, and make us laugh or even cry. These moments are treasures to hold in remembrance, gems to be enjoyed anytime.

There is one very important thing to remember about chocolate. To be its best it needs to be tempered. Tempering involves being heated and cooled until the correct consistency and look is achieved. If chocolate is not tempered it will be dull, crumbly, streaky, and have no snap! In our lives we are often heated, cooled, and stirred up. And, hopefully, through this process, we become snappy and shine.

REFLECTION ACTIVITY

Enough talk about chocolate, go find some and treat yourself. No guilt involved.

CLARITY

"A goal is created three times. First as a mental picture. Second, when written down to add clarity and dimension. And third, when you take action towards its achievement."
—Gary Blair

I AM OLD ENOUGH to remember when I sat in the optometrist's chair with a big metal contraption in front of my eyes. "Is this better, or this?" I couldn't tell because they both seemed about the same. Helen Keller said, "The only thing worse than being blind is having sight but no vision." What a profound statement. When was your last vision checkup?

Sometimes our vision is cloudy. It might be because we have listened to the "shouldn't, couldn't, wouldn't, and can't" voices, those strident voices that can cloud our judgement and drown out our dreams. Turn them off!

Sometimes our vision is double. This happens when we haven't taken the time to fully realize the possibilities. How do we correct this? By gaining a clear focus on what we are called to do. Joel A. Barker is quoted as saying, "Vision without action is merely a dream. Action without vision just passes the time. Vision with action can change the world."

Sometimes we are near-sighted. What is right in front of us can block out possibilities. Clear out the underbrush, the daily weeds that grow and obstruct our view of what truly is important. It may not be comfortable, like that big metal device, but it is necessary.

Sometimes we are far-sighted. The goal is so enticing, yet we cannot comprehend the way or the work that it takes to get there. I have taught my students a chorus written by Ron Hamilton, called "Little by Little." It goes like this: "Little by little, inch by inch, by the yard it's hard, by the inch what a cinch! Never stare up the stairs just step up the steps, little by little, inch by inch." Do the work! Dreamers must be doers to accomplish the vision.

REFLECTION QUESTION

Check your vision and see if it needs clearing up. What's the first step you should take?

DIFFICULTY

D IFFICULTY IS DIFFICULT! Not many children or adults want to do something that is hard. And who can blame them? However, difficulties may result in great opportunities and strength.

Several years ago I went to the pharmacy to get my refills. I was sitting outside waiting for my ride when I saw a man slowly and painfully walk into the hospital. Several minutes later I saw him walk out. When I said hi, he stopped and told me his story. He had a devastating accident and was just beginning to walk after about two years. I looked at him, smiled, and said, "Look how far you have come." He looked just a little shocked and said thanks for the reminder. His was a very difficult difficulty, but he wasn't quitting.

Sometimes, when we are going through something drawn out and hard, we forget to remember the achievements we have made. Remembering those makes the difficult seem bearable. Sonia Sotamajor said it very well: "There are uses to adversity, and they don't reveal themselves until tested. Whether it's serious illness, financial hardship, or the simple constraint of parents who speak limited English, difficulty can tap unexpected strengths."

If you are going through some difficulty, remember to rejoice in your accomplishments so far. They don't have to be major. Little accomplishments add up to something big.

REFLECTION ACTIVITY

Think about some accomplishment/achievement you have made recently. Use that to help you continue to work through any difficulty you may be facing.

DIGNITY

"One's dignity may be assaulted, vandalized, and cruelly mocked,
but cannot be taken away unless it is surrendered."
—Michael J. Fox

P ROVERBS 31:25 SAYS, "She is clothed with strength and dignity, and she laughs without fear of the future." How can we do that? We do that by being comfortable in our own skin: having self-respect. Self-respect isn't pride; it is a solid understanding of ourselves, our strengths and weaknesses.

I couldn't say it better than an article from Mayo clinic: "When you have healthy self-esteem it means you have a balanced, accurate view of yourself. For instance, you have a good opinion of your abilities but recognize your flaws. When self-esteem is healthy and grounded in reality, it's hard to have too much of it. Boasting and feeling superior to others around you isn't a sign of too much self-esteem. It's more likely evidence of insecurity and low self-esteem." (https://www.mayoclinic.org/healthy-lifestyle/adult-health/in-depth/self-esteem/art-20047976)

Where does dignity develop? It comes from the experiences, perceptions, and abilities nurtured as we grow. These can either nurture or destroy self-respect. Does that mean you can never have dignity/self-respect? No. I had a friend who was constantly told she was no good, she would never amount to anything, she was ugly, and other damming epitaphs as she was growing up. She realized these were lies and stopped listening to them. Pamela Meyer says, "... A lie has no power whatsoever by its mere utterance. Its power emerges when someone else agrees to believe the lie." My friend worked hard at figuring out who she really was and became an authentic, accomplished woman.

So, to whom have you surrendered your dignity? Who is it that sapped your strength? Who lied and you believed them? When I was working on my master's, I had a teacher that really lit into me and basically called me a liar. I was ready to quit the program. Then my husband said, "You are not quitting!" I realized if I did then the lie was truth. So, friends, don't let the liars win. Don't quit, walk with dignity, understanding you are worthy of respect from yourself and others.

REFLECTION ACTIVITY

Write down the answers to the questions in the last paragraph. Think about them, and consider what you need to do to develop strength and dignity.

EQUALITY

"...All men are created equal"
—Thomas Jefferson
(https://www.archives.gov/founding-docs/declaration-transcript)

A S IDEAL AND NOBLE AS that sounds, is it true? We are not equally gifted. Even those who are gifted in the same area don't necessarily use it the same way. Ansel Adams used his artistic gift to create wonderful black and white photography. Georgia O'Keefe used her artistic gift to create exuberant art on canvas. Both of these highly talented people used the same gift to show the beauty around us, yet each one was a unique talent.

We are not equal in opportunities. Some are blessed with great opportunities, others have to diligently seek out and create opportunities. Still others haven't been blessed with opportunities, so their talent presents itself only to those in their lives. That doesn't diminish their talent.

We are, however, equal in the responsibility to discover, nurture, and use our unique gifts. We do not have the right to remain an undeveloped seed. We need to personally enjoy and develop the gifts regardless of who else may also benefit. If we don't, then we limit our own happiness and fulfillment that comes from using those gifts.

REFLECTION QUESTIONS

What is a talent that I have? How can I increase it and use it for others?

EXTREMITY

"Our extremities are God's opportunities"
—Charles Spurgeon

MERRIAM-WEBSTER DEFINES extremity as "an intense degree; a drastic or desperate act or measure." This definition conjures up scary images of eminent danger, pain, or overwhelming sorrow.

But maybe it shouldn't. Martin Luther King Jr. wrote "Letter from Birmingham Jail" in response to being called an extremist. He was initially disappointed in that label, but the more he thought about it he began to realize it was a compliment. In the letter, he refers to the extreme position of Martin Luther, John Bunyan, Abraham Lincoln, and Thomas Jefferson. These men, as well as others he mentioned, took extreme positions in their stand for equality and righteousness. He then says, "Perhaps the South, the nation and the world are in dire need of creative extremists."

We need to be extreme in our pursuit of justice, our demonstrations of love, and our development of character. We should practice creative extremity with acts of kindness, loving gentleness, and acceptance. Extremity shouldn't, as another definition says, be a "limb of the body," but should embody our way of living.

REFLECTION QUESTIONS

How does your extreme affect others? Is it for their good, or does it repel them?
Do I need to change my approach? How?

FLAMBOYANCY

(OK, I CHEATED, that is not a ty word, but I like it!)

I will freely admit to being prejudiced. I can't stand those tacky pink flamingos people put in their yards. That means, of course, that my family delights in giving me flamingo cards, toy flamingos, and pointing them out whenever possible. I apologize if that hurts your feelings, Don Featherstone. I know you invented them, but did you know there are now more plastic flamingos in the United States than real ones? (https://www.thespruce.com/fun-facts-about-flamingos-385519.) There is something very wrong about that.

Real flamingos, however, are rather amazing. They get their eye-popping red, orange, or pink color because of their diet. They can even be yellow, blue, or green! If they don't get enough of the pigments from their diet, they aren't colorful. So what? Well, if you as a person really want to stand out, you need to fill your life with things that will enhance and advance you.

Flamingos love to be in the company of other flamingos. They feel much safer in a big crowd. Can you imagine the spectacle of one million flamingos flying? Isolation, even in a crowd of people, can be a very dangerous thing. Having a solid group of friends, maybe not a million, increases your feelings of safety and success.

Don't you think flamingos look awkward standing on one leg? Sometimes we feel like that because we can't figure out the next step. When the flamingo is resting on one leg, it is a position of strength. Just because we are not sure where to take the next step in life doesn't make us weak, indecisive, or afraid. It can mean we are securely resting in our own space until the choice is clear.

Flamingos are strong flyers and swimmers, but are most often seen wading on those long legs. That should remind us to stay firmly grounded. They also don't like other birds to invade their space. That should remind us to respect personal boundaries.

Guess what a group of flamingos are called. Yes, a flamboyance! So, put on some colorful clothes, get together with friends, and be flamboyant! No plastic, imitation flamingos allowed.

REFLECTION QUESTION

Is it better to be a flamboyant dresser or have a flamboyant personality?

GENEROSITY

"Real generosity is doing something nice for someone who will never find out."
—*Frank A. Clark*

"Too many have dispensed with generosity in order to practice charity."
—*Albert Camus*

THERE WERE A LOT of interesting quotes about generosity, but I liked how these dovetailed. I am not so sure I would model my life after Frank A. Clark. He was born in 1960 and became a lawyer and politician. He was a racist. So it is amazing to me that he wrote about being generous. He didn't seem to practice it when dealing with people.

Albert Camus is also an interesting individual. He was born in Algeria in 1913. He grew up to become a writer and philosopher, among other things. The short biography I read said he was considered a "moralist," and yet he had many extra marital affairs. He was an advocate of absurdism. Basically, that means "the belief that human beings exist in a purposeless, chaotic universe." What a sad philosophy.

So from these two men, with definite flaws in philosophy and behavior, come quotes that reveal the truth about generosity. Charity, by definition, is usually about giving money. To "practice charity" implies something public, noticed. Generosity is doing something in a quiet, private way that benefits someone you may not even know. Generosity also involves money, but goes beyond that. It can include time, praise, or material goods. And, often it is given anonymously or privately.

Mark 12: 41-44 tells the story about Jesus watching the crowd in the temple. Many rich people came and put in large amounts of money for the offering, making sure everyone noticed them. Then a widow quietly came and put in a very small amount. Jesus said, "Truly I tell you, this poor widow has put more into the treasury than all the others. They all gave out of their wealth; but she, out of her poverty, put in everything—all she had to live on." It's not the amount, it's the attitude that counts. The rich wanted the adulation that came with the giving. The widow wanted to give what she had from gratitude and love. It seems to me, then, that living a generous life results in more contentment, less stress, and a better attitude.

REFLECTION QUESTIONS

Do you live a generous life? Is there anything you can do to be more generous?

GUILTY

"Guilt upon the conscience, like rust upon iron, both defiles and consumes it, gnawing and creeping into it, as that does which at last eats out the very heart and substance of the metal."
—*Robert South*

So, who was Robert South? Well, apparently he was a rather controversial churchman and quite a wit. This is a quote from a book by Mark Noble: "... whilst giving a sermon to Charles II, he observed the entire congregation had gone to sleep - Noble remarks that, "Stopping and changing the tone of his voice, he called thrice to Lord Lauderdale, who, awakened, stood up: 'My Lord' says South very composedly 'I am sorry to interrupt your repose, but I must beg that you will not snore quite so loud, lest you should awaken his majesty,' and then as calmly continued his discourse." (Noble, Mark (1806). *A Biographical History of England, from the Revolution to the End of George I's Reign*; London: W. Richardson; Darton and Harvey; and W. Baynes. p. 101. Wikipedia 4/22/2021)

So what is guilt? The dictionary defines it as "having committed a breach of conduct." But I think it goes beyond that. Have you ever felt guilty when you have really done nothing wrong? I believe the definition should include "having committed a perceived breach of conduct."

How long should I feel guilty? How do I get rid of it? I looked up how to remove rust and there are several methods. You can use vinegar, ketchup, baking soda, and even Coke! But, I think my favorite is toothpaste.

Toothpaste is made to make our breath smell sweeter as well as our teeth to be shiny. We say we are going to polish our teeth. Well, we should also polish ourselves! Guilt will stain us and eat us for as long as we don't deal with it.

Is there someone you need to talk to and tell them about your guilt? Quite a while ago my husband received a call from someone who had wronged him in college. They called to apologize. It was a wrong that had long since been forgiven. What happens if the person won't forgive? Then it becomes their problem, not yours.

Are you feeling guilt about something you can correct? If so, then you need to plan a way to make it right. Is it false guilt? Examine it carefully and see. If it is, get rid of it; it has no place in your life.

Guilt is like a cancer to your soul, but it is curable. Get out the toothpaste and polish it out of your life. Your smile, breath, and soul will shine.

REFLECTION ACTIVITY

Examine what kind of guilt, if any, you may have. What is the first step you need to take to deal with it?

JOCULARITY

"A day without laughter is a day wasted."
—Charlie Chaplin

T HOSE OF US WHO remember M*A*S*H remember Colonel Potter's imitation of Father Mulcahy saying "Jocularity, Jocularity." It makes us laugh just to remember that episode. And that is exactly what jocularity is. It means "characterized by joking."

Laughter, joking, and having fun are necessary ingredients for a good life. Mark Twain said, "The human race has one really effective weapon, and that is laughter." Laughter can diffuse a tense situation, release anger, lift the spirits, and make an unpleasant situation more tolerable.

Laughter works best when we can laugh at ourselves, not at the expense of others. Medical experts agree that laughter can improve and prolong living. We need a good dose of it every day, just like vitamins.

Laughter is not the small upturn of the lips, or the silent rise of the shoulders. To get the full effect of this vital ingredient to life we need to scrunch up our eyes, shake the shoulders repeatedly, open the mouth to show teeth, and belt out a good "ha-ha." If you can't do that, then start with a little giggle, then proceed to a chortle, then a small laughter, then an outright huge, belly laugh. It is an exercise we should do every day. In fact, start right now! Think of a funny word like "guffaw" and begin. Repeat as often as necessary to give yourself laugh lines.

REFLECTION QUESTION

How can I add more laughter in my life?

LUMINOSITY

"The sun doesn't determine the brightness of the day, you do."
—Kayle Mueller

N OLD CHILDREN'S SONG starts with these words, "This little light of mine, I'm going to let it shine...." Light stimulates life. However, the word luminosity hints at something more. It is defined as "the relative brightness of something."

That suggests that the light is shining through the object. The light is not coming from another source, but is actually coming from the object. We are the light and are projecting it to the world around us.

Some of us, I fear, are not projecting much light! Some of us are wearing shades that dim and diffuse that light. John Steinbeck described a woman in his book *Travels with Charley: In Search of America*, like this: "Strange how one person can saturate a room with vitality, with excitement. Then there are others, and this dame was one of them, who can drain off energy and joy, can suck pleasure dry and get no sustenance from it. Such people spread grayness in the air around them."

Does that sound like anyone you know? Does that sound like you? What a challenge that presents. There are no acceptable excuses. If we are not projecting light to others, then we are projecting darkness. If others aren't energized and sustained by us, we are increasing the lifelessness in the world.

> *This world is filled with enough sorrow, despair, and hope-lessness. We need to let our lights shine brightly.*
> *—(Matthew 6:18)*

REFLECTION QUESTIONS

Why would someone tell you that you are filled with light?
What are ways you could exhibit more luminosity?

PAUCITY

N O, THIS WORD DOES not mean a city of dogs or cats! This word is from the Latin word for little. It means something in a small amount, scarcity. So, let's think about this today.

P Patience
"Patience is not simply the ability to wait—it's how we behave while we're waiting." —Joyce Meyer

A Awareness
"Manners are a sensitive awareness of the feelings of others. If you have that awareness, you have good manners, no matter what fork you use." —Emily Post

U Understanding
"Anger and intolerance are the enemies of correct understanding." —Mahatma Gandhi

C Courtesy
"A tree is known by its fruit; a man by his deeds. A good deed is never lost; he who sows courtesy reaps friendship, and he who plants kindness gathers love." —Saint Basil

I Inclusion
"I believe it's our responsibility to show our communities the value of all people, to celebrate different, and to take a stand for acceptance and inclusion." —Julie Foudy

T Tenacity
"I live by two words: tenacity and gratitude." —Henry Winkler

Y Yippee!
"The secret of genius is to carry the spirit of the child into old age, which means never losing your enthusiasm." —Aldous Huxley

REFLECTION QUESTIONS

Look over the words and quotes you just read. Are any of these scarce in your life? If so, what can you do to eliminate that paucity? Think of the first steps you should make and make them! The teapot you see is made from woven reeds. Although it might hold some, there might be a paucity!

PERPETUITY

"Legacy is not what I did for myself. It's what I'm doing for the next generation."
—Vitor Belfort

THIS WORD IS ACTUALLY a financial term meaning "going on forever." But in thinking about this word, I couldn't help but realize that most of us want to "go on" after our death, but we call it "leaving a legacy."

My husband and I retired from education after over 45 years of being a teacher and/or principal. In our retirement party, one of our students told us that they, all our students, were our legacy. What a precious thought that is. Our legacy is what we poured into our students during all those years. And, we have lived it long enough to see that our students have passed it on to their children.

So, what are you teaching others? Everyone teaches. We teach others by our words. So, do your words encourage, strengthen, or challenge? Or do they denigrate or dismiss?

We also teach by example. So, how do you example life? Do you bully? Do you teach self-centeredness? Do you teach hypocrisy? Do you teach integrity? How about honesty even when it hurts? Are we teaching that others have value even if they are different than us? Disagreement with issues doesn't make others of any less value. All individuals contribute, all are worthy, all should be valued. Some legacies will go on for generations, and others are more fleeting, like a snow angel, but still have an impact on the world.

> *"The greatest legacy one can pass on to one's children and grand-
> children are not money or other material things accumulated
> in one's life, but rather a legacy of character and faith."*
> —Billy Graham

REFLECTION ACTIVITY

There are lots of questions in this reading. Take one and write down your thoughts.

PERSNICKETY

W HEN I VISUALIZE THIS WORD, I see a person, wrapped in self-righteousness, with haughty, condemning eyes and a small, puckered-up mouth, looking down on others. I am sure you have at least one in your life. The first definition of persnickety is fussy, someone who majors on the minors. But, persnickety also means "requiring great precision."

A 125 million dollar Mars space probe crashed and burned because someone didn't check the work. Propulsion engineers typically express force in pounds, but usually convert to newtons for space missions. Engineers at NASA assumed the conversion had been made, and didn't check. (https://www.simscale.com/blog/2017/12/nasa-mars-climate-orbiter-metric/

A chef needs to be precise. There is a poem by an unknown author that gives us the hilarious results. After all the substitutions the writer made to the recipe, the poem ends with, "My friend gave me the recipe—she said you couldn't beat it. There must be something wrong with her, I couldn't even eat it."

Take a good look at the picture of the teapot. Notice that maybe we weren't as persnickety as we should have been!

REFLECTION ACTIVITY

Deliberately choose to live today precisely. Expect experiences that will stretch you, frustrate you, or maybe even leave you awestruck. Meet them head on, intentionally, and draw every ounce of energy from them to make you stronger. Expand your horizons and look for someone who could use some of the wisdom and knowledge you have.

RELATIVITY

IMAGINE WANTING TO KNOW how a tree behaves in a storm, so climbing up one and clinging to it for dear life as a storm rages! Or decide to perch precariously on a rock while Yosemite Falls rushes by. John Muir's appetite for learning about nature was almost insatiable. His books are insightful and inspiring. As interesting as it would be to talk to him, I'd also like to talk to his wife, Louie Stentzel Muir.

Louie, an accomplished musician and excellent student, lived with her parents after her school years. During that time, she learned a great deal about growing fruits and flowers from her horticultural father. When John Muir went on his explorations, she very capably managed their ranch and finances. She chose to do these things rather than travel with her husband. In fact, she once tried camping with him in Yosemite Valley and it was rather disastrous!

We get a glimpse into the kind of relationship they had in a letter she wrote in 1888. "Dear John, A ranch that needs and takes the sacrifice of a noble life or work, ought to be flung away beyond all reach...The Alaska book and the Yosemite book, dear John, must be written and you need to be your own self, well and strong to make them worthy of you." She began downsizing their ranch to help him better focus on his passion for discovery.

Their life together demonstrates what the old-fashioned word helpmate is, partners in the true sense. Louie lived life exercising her strengths, which enabled John to live and use his. Their kind of relationship could be applied in all areas of life. Imagine what changes could be accomplished in our world if we lived our lives doing what we do best, encouraging and supporting others to do their best. It wouldn't matter who got the credit or who was in the spotlight. Either position is vital to success. As Bette Middler said, "You are the wind beneath my wings."

REFLECTION QUESTION

Who can you make their best by being at your best? Think of one way to accomplish this.

RELIABILITY

"Facts from paper are not the same as facts from people. The reliability of the people giving you the facts is as important as the facts themselves."
—*Harold Geneen*

W E DON'T LIKE THAT WORD! It sounds dreary and uninteresting. Maybe we should try consistency, even though it is not a "ty" word. But it is a confusing word! Our minds can go to the quote, "consistency is a hobgoblin of little minds." However, that is not all of the quote. Emerson actually said, "A foolish consistency is the hobgoblin of little minds, adored by little statesmen and philosophers and divines." So is reliability (consistency) foolish, or is there foolish consistency?

We have the capacity to be consistently foolish. And, we aren't the only ones. I grew up on a ranch in Northern California. I remember watching one of my young calves walk into a live electric fence seven times, getting zapped every time, until he got the message that he couldn't reach that lovely green grass on the other side of the fence! He was reliably consistent, but foolish!

We can keep doing the same things over and over. We won't accomplish much and won't necessarily improve. If, however, if we learn from our mistakes and change our methods, we may accomplish more than our original goal.

Bruce Springsteen says, "Getting an audience is hard. Sustaining an audience is hard. It demands a consistency of thought, of purpose, and of action over a long period of time." In other words, we have to be consistently reliable, and that takes courage. That courage is what it takes to keep developing body, soul, and spirit regardless of any challenges or difficulties.

REFLECTION QUESTIONS

Am I reliable? Is it a good type of reliability, or is it something that negatively affects me and those around me?

SERENDIPITY

*"Sometimes life drops blessings in your lap without
your lifting a finger. Serendipity, they call it."*
—*Charles Heston*

I SN'T SERENDIPITY A FUN WORD? It's fun to say and implies the delightfully unexpected happenings in life. It's those things in life that surprise, amaze, and benefit us. Do we look for those things?

Recently I was wandering in an antique/everything store. Since I have had quite a bit of experience with rocks, including agates, I figured I was fairly knowledgeable. But the owner gave me a lesson in serendipity. He picked up an ordinary black rock, the common kind you find along the western coast. Then he took his small flashlight and shined it through the rock. Wow! It was an agate. He taught me an amazing lesson in expecting the unexpected from what might look ordinary.

I thought about a student in my class who really struggled with communication. One of the assignments was to give a short speech about someone who made an impact on the world. Truthfully, I wasn't expecting much from him because of his disability. When it was his turn, he stood tall in front of the class and gave an excellent speech in a loud, clear voice. I sat at my desk and cried as I watched him. And, my class gave him a big round of applause when he finished. It was one of the best speeches that year.

We should live life cherishing and rejoicing in the unexpected. Driving in a rainstorm?

Roll the window down a bit and smell the rain as it hits the hot pavement. Or maybe look for a rainbow. Go outside and listen when it is snowing. There is a calming, beautiful silence. And sometimes snow makes a soft shushing sound as it falls.

The dictionary defines serendipity as "the occurrence and development of events by chance in a happy or beneficial way." (https://www.lexico.com/en/definition/serendipity) Although that is correct, it is maybe not totally accurate. To me, serendipity is a happy occurrence or event that results from living life fully engaged and aware.

REFLECTION QUESTIONS

What was the last serendipitous moment you had? How long ago was it?

SIMPLICITY

"Simplicity is making the journey of this life with just baggage enough."
—Charles Dudley Warner

S IMPLICITY SHOULD NOT BE confused with dull or ordinary. Simplicity can mean the opposite of duplicity. To be simple is really just to be yourself with no artificial trappings that cover up or blur your authentic self.

Decorator crabs cover themselves with bits of shells, rocks, and other ocean debris in order to disguise themselves. You can't tell what they really are.

We should be simply authentic, and let our true selves shine through. At the same time, however, we should never let our "simple selves" stand in the way of exploration and adventure that result in self-discovery and growth. Dr. Seuss reminds us we should not try to fit in because we are meant to stand out.

REFLECTION QUESTIONS

What one thing do you think of that you are hiding behind?
What is the first step you need to take in ridding yourself of that obstacle?

TECHNICALITY

T HIS WORD BRINGS TO MIND someone who "got off on a technicality." Technicality, in that sense, means a small detail. There is another definition: "The specific details or terms belonging to a particular field." (https://www.lexico.com/en/definition/technicality)

If I apply that to my life I would say, like Shakespeare, "This above all else, to thy own self be true." This means I have to really know myself. My family likes New England clam chowder. I never eat it. Why? Shellfish and I don't do well together. I know that about me. So, it isn't part of my life. If I want a life that is full and meaningful, I must know the technicalities about me. But, at the same time, I shouldn't live my life on the technicalities.

Robert Eliot is quoted saying, "Rule number one is, don't sweat the small stuff. Rule number two is, it's all small stuff." That reminds me of the rock, pebble, and sand experiment. Fill a jar with good-sized rocks. Is it full? Try adding pebbles—they fit! Then add some sand and it will fit also. However, if you fill a jar with sand first and then add pebbles, there won't be much room, if any, for rocks. We need to fill our lives with rocks and pebbles—foundational and important truths about us. Then there won't be much room for those trivial things that won't really matter.

REFLECTION ACTIVITY

Take a sheet of paper and make three columns. One will say rocks, one pebbles, and one sand. Then think about the rocks in your life, those truths that are fundamental and need to stay. Next think about the pebbles, those important things that also need to stay. And finally, think about the sand. Do you need to change some things to a different category? Eliminate some?

Warning: This will take a lot of thought and a fair amount of time, but the result will be a better life.

UTILITY PLUS BEAUTY

"The difference between utility and utility plus beauty is the difference between telephone wires and the spider web."
—Edwin Way Teale

THIS QUOTE REALLY SPOKE to me when I found it. So, take a few seconds and let the quote sink in. We all want to be useful. That is what utility means: to be useful or beneficial. But have you ever thought that usefulness should be coupled with beauty?

I believe beauty, as it is used here, is not the fashionista, fully-made up, model-worthy definition. Not many of us would qualify if that were the case! The beauty mentioned here comes from the soul of a person. Have you ever begun a conversation with someone who is "put together" and discover they have really bad breath? Yep! Have you ever been blown away by the wisdom and kindness of someone the world would not take time to look at? It is a humbling experience.

So life, then, should be lived in a way that combines the usefulness of a telephone wire and the beauty of a spider web. How do we do that? Proverbs gives us a lot of information about words, but I like Proverbs 15:23. It says, "A person finds joy in giving an apt reply—and how good is a timely word!"

"A few good words don't just make your day but they also give the sense of belonging and confidence to take the next big step forward." Ravi Shastri. I looked up Mr. Shastri and most of the online biography was about his cricket career. Seriously? When a man has this kind of wisdom, why concentrate on how well he played a game? The biography concentrated on his utility, but totally ignored his beauty. And, from this quote, it seems like there were those in his life who modeled utility with beauty.

That's how we should be living our lives. Useful, yes, and also full of soul beauty. The picture for this is a tea ball, used to keep the tea leaves out of the tea. The straw is used by South American cowboys to keep the tea leaves out of their tea. Utility plus beauty!

REFLECTION QUESTIONS

Who was the last person that modeled utility and soul beauty for you?
Who is someone you can model it to?

OPPORTUNITY

"Therefore, as we have opportunity,
let us do good to all people..."
—Galatians 6:10

THERE ARE LOTS OF "TY" WORDS. I started this book by choosing words that spoke to me. My family and friends also gave me ideas. One day I was really stuck, so decided to look up "ty" on the web. Oh my goodness, there are so many it was overwhelming. Eric Hoffer reminds us that "unlimited opportunities can be as potent a cause of frustration as a ... lack of opportunities."

So what do we do when faced with too many choices? Well, what do you do when you are faced with all the choices at a salad bar? I actually pretend to taste them and see if that is what I really like. Then I fill my plate! Hesitation is not necessarily a bad thing. However, don't miss an opportunity to do something because of doubt. Weigh the consequences and then take a leap!

There are many choices to be made every day. Some we can do almost automatically and others take some thought. But we should never live our lives afraid of the opportunities that come our way. They may lead to exciting difficulties and rewarding pleasures.

You might be saying, "But what if I choose wrong"? By whose standards is it wrong? And, if you find out it was wrong, can't you do something to change? Don't live your life with "if only." That leads to developing the victim mentality. I found this quote from Peter McWilliams: "Definition of a victim: a person to whom life happens." Does life happen to you or are you using every opportunity to live life to the fullest?

Robert Redford has said, "I have no regrets, because I've done everything I could to the best of my ability." Hunter S. Thompson has a saying about life that ends with "thoroughly used up, totally worn out, and loudly proclaiming 'Wow, what a ride!" That is making the most of every opportunity.

REFLECTION ACTIVITY

Consciously look for opportunities as you go through your day and see where they take you. What was the best one? How are you going to change the one you missed?

APPENDIX

HISTORY OF TEA

The year is 2732 BC. According to one legend, Emperor Shen Nung is boiling a pot of water outside. A wind blew some leaves from a wild tree into the pot and we had tea! Although originally used as a medicine, it began to be enjoyed for the pleasant taste. In 780 AD. Lu Yan wrote a book detailing the techniques for growing, harvesting, and drinking tea. He is known as the "Father of Tea." Eventually, tea production moved to other Asian countries and then around the world. The top five producers today are China, India, Kenya, Sri Lanka, Indonesia, and Vietnam (yourbestdip.com). Today there are over 1000 varieties of tea (www.statista.com).

Most Americans are familiar with the Boston Tea Party, when approximately 92,000 pounds of tea were dumped into the harbor. (www.bostonteapartyship.com). However, Joseph Cummins has written an interesting book entitled *Ten Tea Parties: Patriotic Protests That History Forgot* that details other such protests in the colonies.

Do these few facts give you a taste for the history of tea? Have fun learning about it.

HOW TO MAKE A PERFECT CUP OF HOT TEA

The process to making tea is fairly simple. Firstly, you fill your tea kettle with fresh, cold water and bring it to a boil. Don't over boil as that reduces oxygen and makes the tea flat. Use some of the water to rinse and heat the teapot. Put the teabags or loose tea in the teapot and add the water. Steep (let the tea rest in the water) at least five minutes. Don't go by color because flavor is developed slower than color. Pour yourself a cup, adding any other ingredients you like with your tea. Then sit down and enjoy the aroma and flavor!

MAKING ICED TEA

Here's where you could get in trouble, because it's made several different ways. Basic iced tea is made by boiling cold water in a saucepan and then adding teabags to make a concentrated brew. Then add water and ice to make your personal brew strength.

Sweet iced tea is a favorite drink of many. Recipes vary, but basically you make a strong tea, add sugar, and then cool it down. I even found one recipe that used a little bit of baking soda in the water!

Then there is sun tea! Fill a clear gallon jug with cold water and put in up to 8 tea bags. Leave it in the sun for 3-5 hours and then refrigerate. Take out the teabags if you want. This tea is mellower and lasts for about 2 or 3 days.

MY FAVORITE TEA MEMORY

Do you have a favorite memory involving tea? Let me tell you mine.

When my mom was 80 years old, she decided to move to Hawaii to live with some friends. My two sisters and I went over awhile after she moved to spend the week with her. Early in the visit we ate at an excellent beachside restaurant that served deliciously flavored iced tea.

For the rest of the week we stopped everywhere we went to look for the tea and couldn't find it. In desperation, we went back to the restaurant and they gave us a sample with the box. Imagine my surprise when we discovered the tea was manufactured in California, my home state!

Sometimes we run around looking for that certain thing, only to realize it is actually very close to home!

I still enjoy that special tea and think of Mom and that trip with each sip. ☺

What about you? What is your favorite tea moment or memory?

FINAL WORD

I HOPE YOU HAVE been encouraged and challenged as you read through this book. And I hope you enjoyed the pictures. Our prayer and hope is that you make your life one that is worthy of the person you are.

Warmly,

Elda and Andy Robinson

Quotes from this book can be found at www.brainyquotes.com

Quote about Louie Muir comes from Louie Strentzel Muir Biography, John Muir Exhibit, vault.sierraclub.org.

ABOUT THE AUTHOR

ELDA ROBINSON WAS BORN and raised in a small town in Northern California. After graduation from what is now Corban University in Salem, Oregon, she and her husband moved to Wisconsin to work at a care facility for mentally challenged children and adults.

After seven years they moved back to Northern California and began careers in Christian school education. She began her career teaching first grade and music. But, during her 46 plus years, she has taught every grade level. She also served as an elementary principal. In 2009 she received the American Heart Association's Principal of the Year award for her work with Jump Rope for Heart.

She completed her master's degree in Curriculum Development from University of Phoenix in order for her to improve her skills in creating classroom unit studies. She has participated in several conferences as a speaker, including NTTI and ACSI, as well as coauthored a science curriculum that is currently being used in private schools worldwide. She has self-published a children's book called *Nathanial's Family*. Her *Simple Cup of -Ty* book was written as a tribute to her much loved cousin.

She retired from teaching in 2020 and has moved to the central Oregon coast. She can be contacted at bowtieshoes21@gmail.com. She and Andy are contemplating what book may be in the future.

ABOUT THE PHOTOGRAPHER

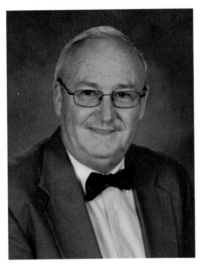

ANDY ROBINSON WAS RAISED in Illinois. After graduating from high school, he attended college at what is now Corban University in Salem, Oregon. One of his goals was to work in television, which he did during his college career. After college, he and Elda moved to Wisconsin to work at a care facility for mentally challenged children and adults, which was another goal. He became a much-loved P.E. teacher and counselor. He and Elda worked there for seven years before moving back to Northern California to begin teaching.

Andy obtained his master's degree in Educational Administration from Pensacola Christian School while he was teaching and being principal at Paradise Christian School in Paradise, California. He then moved on to being the Middle School Principal at Monte Vista Christian School in Watsonville, California. During his time there he was also "the voice of the Mustangs." He enjoyed taking pictures of the scenic ocean around the Monterey Bay.

He and Elda moved to the Bay Area of California in 2008 and worked in Christian schools as teachers and principals until their retirement in 2020. He attended the Columbia Fine Arts Show in Columbia, California selling several of his pictures. He also participated in several local art shows.

After retiring in 2020 he and his wife retired to the central Oregon coast. He can be contacted at bowtieshoes21@gmail.com

REVIEWS

"A Simple Cup of -Ty is a timeless book that fills the mind with wise perspective, centers the heart on what matters most, and lifts the spirit. Keep a copy near you. You'll want to read its interactive pages again and again, because each time you consider Elda's words, you'll rediscover insights on a life well-lived."

 —Shelby Kottemann, Author
 Facebook: Shelby Kottemann
 Instagram: Shelby Kottemann
 shelbykottemann.com (website coming soon)

"Elda Robinson has penned a fantastic book filled with reminders to help develop the lives of everyone who reads *A Simple Cup of -Ty*. I love how each reminder provides the definition with insight, understanding and a challenge to employ each in our daily lives. I highly recommend this book to everyone young and old alike. You will be enriched and inspired!"

 —Donny Ingram
 Author of *Real Freedom*
 https://donnyingram.com

"Elda Robinson's *A Simple Cup of -Ty* is a concise set of essays filled with perfect daily reminders to enhance one's life. Like a perfect cup of tea, not too much, and balanced with inspiration, clarity, and insight, to evoke and bring forth, the best each of us have to offer."
—Maureen Ryan Blake
Founder of The Power of the Tribe Network
https://thepowerofthetribe.com

"What a refreshing read! *A Simple Cup of -Ty* is the perfect volume of whimsical musings and daily inspirations, with action prompts for the reader to apply the wisdom they have gleaned in their own life. Thanks for sharing this delightful work."
—Aeriol Ascher
Author/Coach
www.aeriolascher.com

"A delightful way to start or end your day, *A Simple Cup of -Ty* is the ideal book to set your intentions and provide guidance for how and why we make choices in our life. The powerful compilation of important messages is both heart-felt and meaningful. The author, Elda Robinson, shares her inspiration and compassion with all of us, and the readers truly benefit from her insightful support and challenges for improvement. If your hope is to make your life one that is worthy of the person you are, this is the perfect book for you!"
—Wendy K. Benson, MBA, OTR/L and Elizabeth A. Myers, RN
Co-Authors, *The Confident Patient*
2x2 Health: Private Health Concierge, http://www.2x2health.com/